The Sibbetts

Merry Xmas — 1968

Lottie Bruce

THE GREATEST THING
IN THE WORLD

THE GREATEST THING IN THE WORLD

Henry Drummond's Inspirational Classic
In a Modern, Readable Edition,
With Other Selected Essays

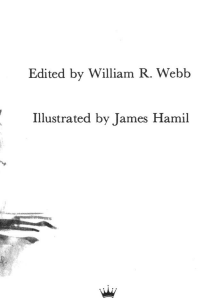

Edited by William R. Webb

Illustrated by James Hamil

HALLMARK EDITIONS

Contents

THE GREATEST THING
IN THE WORLD

The Greatest Thing in the World

Though I speak with the tongues of men and of angels, and have not love, I am become as sounding brass, or a tinkling cymbal. And though I have the gift of prophecy, and understand all mysteries, and all knowledge; and though I have all faith, so that I could remove mountains, and have not love, I am nothing. Love suffereth long, and is kind; love envieth not; love vaunteth not itself, is not puffed up, doth not behave itself unseemly, seeketh not her own, is not easily provoked, thinketh no evil; Rejoiceth not in iniquity, but rejoiceth in the truth; Beareth all things, believeth all things, hopeth all things, endureth all things.

Love never faileth: but whether there be prophecies, they shall fail; whether there be tongues, they shall cease; whether there be knowledge, it shall vanish away. For we know in part, and we prophesy in part. But when that which is perfect is come, then that which is in part shall be done away.

And now abideth faith, hope, love, these three; but the greatest of these is love.

— 1 Corinthians 13

7

We are accustomed to being told that the greatest thing in the religious world is Faith. That great word has been the keynote for centuries of the popular religion; and we have easily learned to look upon it as the greatest thing in the world. Well, we are wrong. I take you to Christianity at its source; and there we see, "The greatest of these is love."

Paul says, "If I have all faith, so that I can remove mountains, and have not love, I am nothing." He deliberately contrasts them, "Now abideth faith, hope, love" and without a moment's hesitation, the decision falls, "The greatest of these is love."

The masterpieces of Christianity are agreed about it. Peter says, "Above all things have fervent love among yourselves." *Above all things.* And John goes farther, "God is love." And you remember the profound remark which Paul

9

makes, "Love is the fulfilling of the law." Did you ever think what he meant by that? In those days men were working their passage to Heaven by keeping the Ten Commandments, and the hundred and ten other commandments which they had manufactured out of them. Christ said, I will show you a more simple way. If you do one thing, you will do these hundred and ten things, without ever thinking about them. If you love, you will unconsciously fulfill the whole law.

Take any of the commandments. "Thou shalt have no other gods before Me." If a man love God, you will not have to tell him that. Love is the fulfilling of that law. "Take not His name in vain." Would he ever dream of taking His name in vain if he loved Him? "Remember the Sabbath day to keep it holy." Would he not be too glad to have one day in seven to dedicate more exclusively to the object of his affection? Love would fulfill all these laws regarding God. And so, if he loved Man, you would never think of telling him to honor his father and mother. He could not do anything else. It would be preposterous to tell him not to kill. You could only insult him if you suggested that he should not steal — how could he steal from those he loved? It would be superfluous to beg him not to bear false witness against his neighbor. If he loved him it would be the last thing he would do. And you would never dream of urging him not to covet what his neighbors had. He would rather they possessed it than himself. In this way, "Love is the fulfilling of the law." It is the rule for fulfilling all rules, the new commandment for keeping all the old commandments, Christ's one secret of the Christian life.

Paul contrasts love with eloquence. And what a noble gift it is, the power of playing upon the souls and wills of men, and rousing them to lofty purposes and holy deeds. Paul says, "If I speak with the tongues of men and of angels, and have not love, I am become as sounding brass, or a tinkling cymbal." And we all know why. We have all felt the brazenness of words without emotion, the hollowness, the unaccountable unpersuasiveness of eloquence behind which lies no Love.

Paul contrasts love with faith. He contrasts it with charity. Why is love greater than faith? Because the end is greater than the means. And why is it greater than charity? Because the whole is greater than the part. Love is greater than faith, because the end is greater than the means. What is the use of having faith? It is to connect the soul with God. And what is the object of connecting man with God? That he may become

11

like God. But God is Love. Hence Faith, the means, is in order to love, the end. Love, therefore, is obviously greater than faith. It is greater than charity, again, because the whole is greater than a part. Charity is only a little bit of love, one of the innumerable avenues of love, and there may even be, and there is, a great deal of charity without love.

Paul passes this thing, love, through the magnificent prism of his inspired intellect, and it comes out broken up into its elements. And in his words we have what one might call the spectrum of love, the analysis of love.

The spectrum of love has nine ingredients:

PATIENCE	*"Love suffereth long."*
KINDNESS	*"And is kind."*
GENEROSITY	*"Love envieth not."*
HUMILITY	*"Love vaunteth not itself, is not puffed up."*
COURTESY	*"Doth not behave itself unseemly."*
UNSELFISHNESS	*"Seeketh not her own."*
GOOD TEMPER	*"Is not easily provoked."*
GUILELESSNESS	*"Thinketh no evil."*
SINCERITY	*"Rejoiceth not in iniquity, but rejoiceth in truth."*

Patience;   kindness;   generosity;   humility;

courtesy; unselfishness; good temper; guilelessness; sincerity — these make up the supreme
gift, the stature of the perfect man. You will ob-
serve that all are in relation to men, in relation
to life, in relation to the known today and the
near tomorrow, and not to the unknown eterni-
ty. We hear much of love of God; Christ spoke
much of love of man. We make a great deal of
peace with Heaven; Christ made much of peace
on earth. Religion is not a strange or added
thing, but the inspiration of the secular life, the
breathing of an eternal spirit through the tem-
poral world. The supreme thing, in short, is not
a thing at all, but the giving of a further finish
to the multitudinous words and acts which make
up the sum of every common day.

Love is PATIENCE. This is the normal attitude
of love; love passive, love waiting to begin; not
in a hurry; calm; ready to do its work when the
summons comes but meantime wearing the or-
nament of a meek and quiet spirit. Love suffers
long; beareth all things; believeth all things;
hopeth all things. For love understands, and
therefore waits.

KINDNESS. Give pleasure. Lose no chance of
giving pleasure. For that is the ceaseless and
anonymous triumph of a truly loving spirit. "I
will pass through this world but once. Any good

thing therefore that I can do, or any kindness that I can show to any human being, let me do it now. Let me not defer it or neglect it, for I shall not pass this way again."

GENEROSITY. "Love envieth not." That most despicable of all the unworthy moods which cloud a Christian's soul assuredly waits for us on the threshold of every work, unless we are fortified with this grace of magnanimity. And then, after having learned that, you have to learn this further thing, HUMILITY — to put a seal upon your lips and forget what you have done.

Love hides even from itself. Love waives even self-satisfaction. "Love vaunteth not itself, is not puffed up."

COURTESY. This is love in society, love in relation to etiquette. "Love doth not behave itself unseemly." Politeness has been defined as love in trifles. Courtesy is said to be love in little things. And the one secret of politeness is to love. Love *cannot* behave itself unseemly. You can put the most untutored persons into the highest society, and if they have a reservoir of love in their hearts, they will not behave themselves unseemly. They simply cannot do it.

Carlyle said of Robert Burns that there was no truer gentleman in Europe than the ploughman-poet. It was because he loved everything — the mouse, and the daisy, and all the things, great and small, that God had made. So with this simple passport he could mingle with any society, and enter courts and palaces from his little cottage on the banks of the Ayr.

UNSELFISHNESS. "Seekest thou great things for thyself?" said the prophet: *"seek them not."* Why? Because there is no greatness in *things.* Things cannot be great. The only greatness is unselfish love. Even self-denial in itself is nothing, is almost a mistake. Only a great purpose or a mightier love can justify the waste.

The most obvious lesson in Christ's teaching is that there is no happiness in having and getting anything, but only in giving. I repeat, *there is no happiness in having, or in getting, but only in giving.* And half the world is on the wrong scent in the pursuit of happiness. They think it consists in having and getting, and in being served by others. It consists in giving and serving others. "He that would be great among you," said Christ, "let him serve." He that would be happy, let him remember that there is but one way — it is more blessed, it is more happy, to give than to receive.

GOOD TEMPER. "Love is not easily provoked." The compatibility of ill temper with high moral character is one of the strangest and saddest

16

problems of ethics. The truth is there are two great classes of sins — sins of the *Body,* and sins of the *Disposition.* The Prodigal Son may be taken as a type of the first, the Elder Brother of the second.

For embittering life, for breaking up communities, for destroying the most sacred relationships, for devastating homes, for withering up men and women, for taking the bloom off childhood; in short, for sheer gratuitous misery-producing power, this influence stands alone. Look at the Elder Brother, moral, hard-working, patient, dutiful — let him get all credit for his virtues — look at this man, this baby, sulking outside his own father's door. "He was angry," we read, "and would not go in." Look at the effect upon the father, upon the servants, upon the happiness of the guests. Judge the effect upon the Prodigal — and how many prodigals are kept out of the Kingdom of God by the unlovely characters of those who profess to be inside?

What is temper made of? Jealousy, anger, pride, uncharity, cruelty, self-righteousness, touchiness, doggedness, sullenness — these are the ingredients of this dark and loveless soul. In varying proportions, also, these are the ingredients of all ill temper.

Temper is a test for love, a symptom, a revela-

17

tion of an unloving nature at bottom. It is the intermittent fever which bespeaks unintermittent disease within; the occasional bubble escaping to the surface which betrays some rottenness underneath; a sample of the most hidden products of the soul dropped involuntarily when off one's guard; in a word, the lightning form of a hundred hideous and un-Christian sins. For a want of patience, a want of kindness, a want of generosity, a want of courtesy, a want of unselfishness, are all instantaneously symbolized in one flash of temper.

GUILELESSNESS. The possession of guilelessness is the great secret of personal influence. You will find, if you think for a moment, that the people who influence you are people who believe in you. In an atmosphere of suspicion men shrivel up; but in an atmosphere of love they expand and find encouragement and educative fellowship. It is a wonderful thing that here and there in this hard, uncharitable world there should still be left a few rare souls who think no evil. This is the great unworldliness. Love "thinketh no evil," imputes no motive, sees the bright side, puts the best construction on every action.

SINCERITY. What Paul really meant is, as we read, "Rejoiceth not in unrighteousness, but rejoiceth with the truth," a quality which probably

no one English word — and certainly no *Sincerity* — adequately defines. It includes, perhaps more strictly, the self-restraint which refuses to make capital out of others' faults; the charity which delights not in exposing the weakness of others, but "covereth all things"; the sincerity of purpose which endeavors to see things as they are, and rejoices to find them better than suspicion feared or calumny denounced.

Is life not full of opportunities for learning love ? Every man and woman every day has a thousand of them. The world is not a playground; it is a schoolroom. Life is not a holiday, but an education. And the one eternal lesson for us all is *how better we can love.*

If a man does not exercise his arm he develops no biceps muscle; if a man does not exercise his soul, he acquires no muscle in his soul, no strength of character, no vigor of moral fiber, nor beauty of spiritual growth. Love is not a thing of enthusiastic emotion. It is a rich, strong, manly, vigorous expression of the whole round Christian character — the Christ-like nature in its fullest development. And the constituents of this great character are only to be built up by ceaseless practice.

Above all, do not resent temptation; do not be perplexed because it seems to thicken round you more and more, and ceases neither for effort nor for agony nor prayer. That is the practice which God appoints you; and it is having its work in making you patient, and humble, and generous, and unselfish, and kind, and courteous. Do not grudge the hand that is molding the still too shapeless image within you. It is growing more beautiful though you see it not, and every touch of temptation may add to its perfection. Therefore keep in the midst of life.

Remember Goethe's words: "Talent develops itself in solitude; character in the stream of life." Talent develops itself in solitude — the talent of prayer, of faith, of meditation, of seeing the unseen; character grows in the stream of the world's life. That chiefly is where men are to learn love.

Love itself can never be defined. Light is something more than the sum of its ingredients — a glowing, dazzling, tremulous ether. And love is something more than all of its elements — a palpitating, quivering, sensitive, living thing. By synthesis of all the virtues, men can make virtue. They cannot make love. How then are we to have this transcendent living whole conveyed into our souls? We brace our wills to secure it. We try to copy those who have it. We lay down rules about it. We watch. We pray. But these things alone will not bring love into our nature. Love is an *effect*. And only as we fulfill the right condition can we have the effect produced.

Put a piece of iron in the presence of a magnetized body, and that piece of iron for a time becomes magnetized. It is charged with an attractive force in the mere presence of the original force, and as long as you leave the two side by side, they are both magnets alike. Remain side by side with Him who loved us and gave Himself for us, and you too will become a center of power, a permanently attractive force; and like Him you will draw all men unto you, like Him you will be drawn unto all men.

"Love," urges Paul, "never faileth." Then he begins again one of his marvelous lists of the great things of the day, and exposes them one by one. He runs over the things that men thought were going to last, and shows that they are all fleeting, temporary, passing away.

"Whether there be prophecies, they shall fail." It was the mother's ambition for her boy in those days that he should become a prophet. For hundreds of years God had never spoken by means of any prophet, and at that time the prophet was greater than the king. Men waited wistfully for another messenger to come, and hung upon his lips when he appeared as upon the very voice of

22

God. Paul says, "Whether there be prophecies they shall fail."

Then Paul talks about tongues. That was another thing that was greatly coveted. "Whether there be tongues, they shall cease." As we all know, many centuries have passed since tongues have been known in this world. They have ceased. Take it in any sense you like. Take it, for illustration merely, as languages in general — a sense which was not in Paul's mind at all, and which, though it cannot give us the specific lesson, will point the general truth. Consider the words in which Paul wrote — Greek. It has gone. Take the Latin — the other great tongue of those days. It ceased long ago. Look at the Indian language. It is ceasing. The language of Wales, of Ireland, of the Scottish Highlands is dying before our eyes.

Then Paul goes farther, and with even greater boldness adds, "Whether there be knowledge, it shall vanish away." The wisdom of the ancients, where is it? It is wholly gone. A schoolboy today knows more than Sir Isaac Newton knew. His knowledge has vanished away. You put yesterday's paper in the fire. Its knowledge has vanished away. You buy the old editions of the great encyclopedias for a few pence. Their knowledge has vanished away.

Can you tell me anything that is going to last? Many things Paul did not condescend to name. He did not mention money, fortune, fame; but he picked out the great things of his time, the things the best men thought had something in them, and brushed them peremptorily aside. Paul had no charge against these things in themselves. All he said about them was that they would not last. They were great things, but not supreme things.

There is a great deal in the world that is delightful and beautiful; there is a great deal in it that is engrossing; but it will not last. All that is in the world, the lust of the eye, the lust of the flesh, and the pride of life, are but for a little while. Love not the world therefore. Nothing that it contains is worth the life and consecration of an immortal soul. The immortal soul must give itself to something that is immortal. And the only immortal things are these: "Now abideth faith, hope, love, but the greatest of these is love."

Some think the time will come when two of these three things will also pass away — faith into sight, hope into fruition. Paul does not say so. We know but little now about the conditions of the life that is to come. But what is certain is that love must last. God, the Eternal God, is Love. Covet therefore that everlasting gift, that one thing which it is certain is going to stand, that one coinage which will be current in the universe when all the other coinages of all the nations of the world shall be useless and unhonored. You will give yourselves to many things, give yourselves first to love. Hold things in their proportion. *Hold things in their proportion.* Let at least the first great object of our lives be to achieve the character defended in these words, the character, — and it is the character of Christ — which is built around love.

The Gospel offers a man life. Never offer men a thimbleful of Gospel. Do not offer them merely joy, or merely peace, or merely rest, or merely safety; tell them how Christ came to give men a more abundant life than they have, a life abundant in love, and therefore abundant in salvation for themselves, and large in enterprise for the alleviation and redemption of the world. Then only can the Gospel take hold of the whole of a man; body, soul, and spirit, and give to each part of his nature its exercise and reward. Many of the current gospels are addressed only to a part of man's nature. They offer peace, not life; faith, not love; justification, not regeneration. And men slip back again from such religion because it has never really held them.

Eternal life is inextricably bound up with love.

We want to live forever for the same reason that we want to live tomorrow. Why do you want to live tomorrow? It is because there is someone who loves you, and whom you want to see tomorrow, and be with, and love back.

No worse fate can befall a man in this world than to live and grow old alone, unloving and unloved. To be lost is to live in an unregenerate condition, loveless and unloved; and to be saved is to love; and he that dwelleth in love dwelleth already in God. For God is Love.

I have seen almost all the beautiful things that God has made; I have enjoyed almost every pleasure that He has planned for man; and yet as I look back I see standing out above all the life that has gone four or five short experiences when the love of God reflected itself in some poor imitation, some small act of love of mine, and these seem to be things which alone of all one's life abide.

It is the Son of *Man* before whom the nations of the world shall be gathered. It is in the presence of *Humanity* that we shall be charged. And the spectacle itself, the mere sight of it, will silently judge each one. Those will be there whom we have met and helped; or there, the unpitied multitude whom we neglected or despised. No other witness need be summoned.

The words which all of us shall one Day hear sound not of theology, but of life, not of churches and saints but of the hungry and the poor, not of creeds and doctrines but of shelter and clothing, not of Bibles and prayerbooks but of cups of cold water in the name of Christ.

Who is Christ? He who fed the hungry, clothed the naked, visited the sick. And where is Christ? Where? — whoso shall receive a little child in my name receiveth Me. And who are Christ's? Every one that loveth is born of God.

The Changed Life

I protest that if some great Power would agree to make me always think what is true and do what is right, on condition of being turned into a sort of clock and wound up every morning, I think I should instantly close with the offer.

T. H. Huxley

31

These are the words of Mr. Huxley. The infinite desirability, the infinite difficulty of being good — the theme is as old as humanity. The man does not live from whose deeper being the same confession has not risen, or who would not give his all tomorrow, if he could "close with the offer" of becoming a better man.

I propose to make that offer now. In all seriousness, without being "turned into a sort of clock," the end can be attained. Under the right conditions it is as natural for character to become beautiful as for a flower; and if on God's earth there is not some machinery for effecting it, the supreme gift to the world has been forgotten. This is simply what man was made for. With Browning: "I say that man was made to grow, not stop." Or in the deeper words of an older Book: "Whom He did foreknow, He also did predestinate . . . to be conformed to the Image of His Son."

A formula, a recipe, for sanctification — can one seriously speak of this mighty change as if the process were as definite as for the production of so many volts of electricity? It is impossible to doubt it. Shall a mechanical experiment succeed infallibly, and the one vital experiment of humanity remain a chance? Is corn to grow by method, and character by caprice? If we cannot calculate to a certainty that the forces of religion will do their work, then is religion vain? And if we cannot express the law of these forces in simple words, then is Christianity not the world's religion but the world's conundrum?

If we turn to textbooks of Christianity, we shall find a formula for this problem as clear and precise as any in the mechanical sciences. If this simple rule, moreover, be but followed fearlessly, it will yield the result of a perfect character as surely as any result that is guaranteed by the laws of nature. The finest expression of this rule in Scripture, or indeed in any literature, is probably one drawn up and condensed into a single verse by Paul. You will find it in a letter — the second to the Corinthians — written by him to some Christian people who were seeking the

34

higher life. The words are these: "We all, with unveiled face reflecting as a mirror the glory of the Lord, are transformed into the same image from glory to glory, even as from the Lord the Spirit."

In physiology the verbs describing the processes of growth are in the passive. Growth is not voluntary; it takes place, it happens, it is wrought upon matter. So here. "Ye must be born again"— we cannot *born* ourselves. "Be not conformed to this world but *be ye transformed*" — we are subject to a transforming influence, we do not transform ourselves. Not more certain is it that it is something outside the thermometer that produces a change in the thermometer, than it is something outside the soul of man that produces a moral change upon him.

As the branch ascends, and the bud bursts, and the fruit reddens under the cooperation of influences from the outside air, so man arises to the higher stature under invisible pressures from without.

According to the first law of motion: Every body continues in its state of rest, or of uniform motion in a straight line, except in so far as it may be compelled *by impressed forces* to change that state. This is also a first law of Christianity. Every man's character remains as it is, or continues in the direction in which it is going, until it is compelled *by impressed forces* to change that state.

There is a clay, and there is a Potter; we have tried to get the clay to mold the clay.

The answer of the formula is "By reflecting as a mirror the glory of the Lord we are changed." But this is not very clear. What is the "glory" of the Lord, and how can mortal man reflect it, and how can that act as an "impressed force" in molding him to a nobler form? The word "glory" — the word which has to bear the weight of holding those "impressed forces"— is a stranger in current speech, and our first duty is to seek out its equivalent in working English. It suggests at first a radiance of some kind, something dazzling or glittering, some halo such as the old masters loved to paint around the heads of their Ecce Homos. But that is paint, mere matter, the visible symbol of some unseen thing. What is that unseen thing? It is that of all unseen things, the most radiant, the most beautiful, the most divine, and that is *character*. On earth, in Heaven, there is nothing so great, so glorious as this. The word has many meanings; in ethics it can have but one. Glory is character and nothing less, and it can be nothing more. The earth is "full of the glory of the Lord," because it is full

of His character. The "Beauty of the Lord" is character. "The effulgence of His Glory" is character, the character which is "fullness of grace and truth."

Here the solution of the problem of sanctification is compressed into a sentence: Reflect the character of Christ and you will become like Christ.

The mind, the memory, the soul, is simply a vast chamber panelled with looking-glass. And upon this miraculous arrangement and endowment depends the capacity of mortal souls to "reflect the character of the Lord."

The influences we meet are not simply held for a moment on the polished surface and thrown off again into space. Each is retained where first it fell, and stored up in the soul forever.

This law of assimilation is the second, and by far the most impressive truth which underlies the formula of sanctification — the truth that men are not only mirrors, but that these mirrors so far from being mere reflectors of the fleeting things they see, transfer into their own inmost substance, and hold in permanent preservation the things that they reflect.

If events change men, much more persons. No man can meet another on the street without making some mark upon him. We say we exchange words when we meet; what we exchange is souls. And when intercourse is very close and very frequent, so complete is this exchange that recognizable bits of the one soul begin to show in the other's nature, and the second is conscious of a similar and growing debt to the first.

It is the law of influence that *we become like those whom we habitually admire.* On the doctrine of influence, in short, the whole vast pyramid of humanity is built.

It was reserved for Paul to make the supreme application of the law of influence. It was a tremendous inference to make, but he never hesitated. He himself was a changed man; he knew exactly what had done it; it was Christ.

Since we are what we are by the impacts of those who surround us, those who surround themselves with the highest will be those who change into the highest.

To live with Socrates — with unveiled face — must have made one wise; with Aristides, just. Francis of Assisi must have made one gentle; Savonarola, strong. But to have lived with Christ? To have lived with Christ must have made one like Christ; that is to say, *a Christian.*

How can we mirror that which we have never seen? How can all this stupendous result be produced by a memory, by the scantiest of all biographies, by One who lived and left this earth more than nineteen hundred years ago? How can modern men today make Christ, the absent Christ, their most constant companion still? The answer is that friendship is a spiritual thing. It is independent of matter, or space, or time. That which I love in my friend is not that which I see. What influences me in my friend is not his body but his spirit.

All friendship, all love, human and Divine, is purely spiritual. It was after Christ was risen that He influenced even the disciples most. Hence in reflecting the character of Christ it is no real obstacle that we may never have been in visible contact with Him.

Now this is not imitation, but a much deeper thing. Mark this distinction. For the difference in the process, as well as in the result, may be as great as that between a photograph secured by the infallible pencil of the sun, and the rude outline from a schoolboy's chalk. Imitation is mechanical, reflection organic. The one is occasional, the other habitual. In the one case, man comes to God and imitates Him; in the other, God comes to man and imprints Himself upon him.

In looking at a mirror one does not see the mirror, or think of it, but only of what it reflects.

For a mirror never calls attention to itself — except when there are flaws in it.

Do not think that nothing is happening because you do not see yourself grow, or hear the whir of machinery. All great things grow noiselessly. You can see a mushroom grow, but never a child. Mr. Darwin tells us that evolution proceeds by "numerous, successive, and slight modifications." Paul knew that, and put it, only in more beautiful words, into the heart of his formula. He said for the comforting of all slowly perfecting souls that they grew "from character to character." "The inward man," he says elsewhere, "is renewed from day to day."

As the man is to the animal in the slowness of his evolution, so is the spiritual man to the natural man. Foundations which have to bear the weight of an eternal life must be surely laid. Character is to wear forever; who will wonder or grudge that it cannot be developed in a day?

A religion of effortless adoration may be a religion for an angel but never for a man. Not in the contemplative but in the active lies true hope; not in rapture, but in reality lies true life; not in the realm of ideals but among tangible things is man's sanctification wrought.

The Program of Christianity

To preach good tidings unto the meek: To bind up
the broken-hearted: To proclaim liberty to the captives and the opening of the prison to them that are
bound: To proclaim the acceptable year of the
Lord, and the day of vengeance of our God: To
comfort all that mourn: To appoint unto them that
mourn in Zion: To give unto them — beauty for
ashes, the oil of joy for mourning, the garment of
praise for the spirit of heaviness.

— Isaiah 61:1-3

43

What does God do all day?" once asked a little boy. One could wish that more grown-up people would ask so very real a question. Unfortunately, most of us are not even boys in religious intelligence, but only very unthinking children. It no more occurs to us that God is engaged in any particular work in the world than it occurs to a little child that its father does anything except be its father.

Childhood, whether in the physical or moral world, is the great self-centered period of life; and a personal God who satisfies personal ends is all that for a long time many a Christian understands.

But as clearly as there comes to the growing child a knowledge of its father's part in the world, and a sense of what real life means, there must come to every Christian whose growth is

45

true, some richer sense of the meaning of Christianity and a larger view of Christ's purpose for mankind. To miss this is to miss the whole splendor and glory of Christ's religion.

Christ has a purpose for mankind, a purpose beyond man and his needs, beyond the churches and their creeds, beyond heaven and its saints — a purpose which embraces every man and woman born, every kindred and nation formed, which regards not their spiritual good alone but their welfare in every part, their progress, their health, their work, their wages, their happiness in this present world.

The tendency of the religions of all time has been to care more for religion than for humanity; Christ cared more for humanity than for religion — rather, His care for humanity was the chief expression of His religion.

What Christ came here for was to make a better world. The world in which we live is an unfinished world. It is not wise, it is not happy, it is not pure, it is not good — it is not even sanitary. Humanity is little more than raw material. Almost everything has yet to be done to it. Before the days of Geology people thought the earth was finished. It is by no means finished. The work of Creation is going on. Before the spectroscope, men thought the universe was finished. We know it is just beginning. And this teeming universe of men in which we live has almost all its finer color and beauty yet to take. Christ came to complete it.

God's way of making worlds is to make them make themselves. When He made the earth He made a rough ball of matter and supplied it with a multitude of tools to mold it into form — the raindrops to carve it, the glacier to smooth it, the river to nourish it, the flower to adorn it.

Christ's great word was the Kingdom of God. Of all the words of His that have come down to us this is by far the commonest. One hundred times it occurs in the Gospels.

Men repudiate Christ's religion because they think it a small and limited thing, a scheme with no large human interests to commend it to this great social age. I ask you to note that there is not one burning interest of the human race which is not represented here. What are the great words of Christianity!

Take as specimens these: LIBERTY,

COMFORT,

BEAUTY,

JOY.

These are among the greatest words of life. Give them their due extension, the significance which Christ undoubtedly saw in them and which Christianity undoubtedly yields, and there is almost no great want or interest of mankind which they do not cover.

Loveliness does more than destroy ugliness. A mere touch of it in a room, in a street, even on a door knocker, is a spiritual force. Ask the workingman's wife, and she will tell you there is a moral effect even in a clean table-cloth. The mere light and color of the wall advertisements are a gift of God to the poor man's somber world.

Christianity, of all other philanthropies, recognizes that man's devouring need is *Liberty* — liberty to stop sinning; to leave the prison of his passions, and shake off the fetters of his past. To surround *Captives* with statues and pictures, to offer *They-that-are-Bound* a higher wage or a cleaner street or a few more cubic feet of air per head, is solemn trifling. It is a cleaner soul they want; a purer air, or any air at all, for their higher selves.

The old theory that God made the world, made it as an inventor would make a machine, and then stood looking on to see it work, has passed away. God is no longer a remote spectator of the natural world, but immanent in it, pervading matter by His present Spirit, and ordering it by His Will.

Christ is immanent in men. His work is to move the hearts and inspire the lives of men, and through such hearts to move and reach the world. Men, only men, can carry out this work. This humanness, this inwardness, of the Kingdom is one reason why some scarcely see that it exists at all. We measure great movement by the loudness of their advertisement, or the place their externals fill in the public eye. This Kingdom has no externals.

Men *must* live among men. Men *must* influence men. Organizations, institutions, churches, have too much rigidity for a thing that is to flood the world. The only fluid in the world is man. War might have won for Christ's cause a passing victory; wealth might have purchased a superficial triumph; political power might have gained a temporary success. But in these there is no note of universality, of solidarity, of immortality. To live through the centuries and pervade the uttermost ends of the earth, to stand while kingdoms tottered and civilizations changed, to survive fallen churches and crumbling creeds — there was no soil for the Kingdom of God like the hearts of common men.

Some who have written about this Kingdom have emphasized the moral grandeur, others its universality, others its adaptation to man's needs. One great writer speaks of its prodigious originality, another chiefly notices its success. I confess what strikes me most is the miracle of its simplicity.

No man has a right to postpone his *life* for the sake of his thoughts. Why? Because this is a real world, not a *think* world. Treat it as a real world — act. Think by all means, but think also of what is actual.

It too seldom occurs to those who repudiate Christianity because of its narrowness or its unpracticalness, its sanctimoniousness or its dullness, that these were the very things which Christ strove against and unweariedly condemned. It was the one risk of His religion being given to the common people — an inevitable risk which He took without reserve — that its infinite luster should be tarnished in the fingering of the crowd or have its great truths narrowed into mean and unworthy molds as they passed from lip to lip.

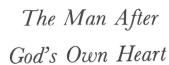

The Man After
God's Own Heart

A man after mine own heart,
who shall fulfill all my will.
— *Acts 13:22*

No man can be making much of his life who has not a very definite conception of what he is living for. And if you ask, at random, a dozen men what is the end of their life, you will be surprised to find how few have formed more than the most dim idea.

The Christian must have a definite aim and model for his life. His one book has taught him a nobler life than all the libraries of the rich and immortal past. He may wish to be a man of business, or a man of science, and indeed he may be both. But he covets a nobler name than these. He will be the man after God's own heart. He has found out the secret philosophy, that the ideal life is this — "A man after mine own heart, who shall fulfill all my will."

He is a great man who has a great plan for his life — the greatest who has the greatest plan and keeps it. And the Christian should have the greatest plan, as his life is the greatest, as his work is the greatest, as his life and his work will follow him when all this world's is done.

What is the true plan of the Christian life? We shall need a definition that we may know it, a description that we may follow it. And if you look, you will see that both, in a sense, lie on the surface of the text. "A man after mine own heart" — here is the definition of what we are to be. "Who shall fulfill my will" — here is the description of how we are to be it. These words are the definition and the description of the model human life.

One will tell you the end of life is to be true. Another will tell you it is to deny self. Another will say it is to keep the Ten Commandments. A fourth will point you to the Beatitudes. One will tell you it is to *do* good, another that it is to *get* good, another that it is to *be* good. But the end of life is in none of these things. It is more than all, and it includes them all. The end of life is not to deny self, nor to be true, nor to keep the Ten Commandments — it is simply to do God's will.

The great philosophers, from Socrates and

Plato to Immanuel Kant and Mill, have given us their conception of an ideal human life. Each of them has constructed an ideal human life, a universal life they call it, a life for all other lives, a life for all men and all time to copy. None of them is half so deep, so wonderful, so far-reaching, as this: "A man after mine own heart, who shall fulfill all my will."

What is meant by telling a man to follow Christ? How is it to be done? It is like putting a young artist before a Murillo or a Raphael, and telling him to copy it. But even as the artist in following his ideal has colors put into his hand, and brush and canvas, and a hint here from his master, and a touch there from another, so with the pupil in the school of Christ. The Great Master Himself is there to help him. The Holy Spirit is there to help him. But the model of life is not to be mystically attained. There is spirituality about it, but no reality. So God has provided another great help, our second help: the Model Life analyzed in the Word of God. Without the one, the ideal life would be incredible; without the other, it would be unintelligible. Hence God has given us two sides of this model life: realized in the Living Word; analyzed in the written Word.

BIOGRAPHICAL NOTE

Henry Drummond
(1851-1897)

Henry Drummond, the Scottish scientist-evangelist, first gave his famous inspirational lecture "The Greatest Thing in the World" in 1883 at a mission station in Central Africa. The Rev. Dwight L. Moody heard Drummond's talk the following year and said he had "never heard anything so beautiful." Based on the Bible's "love chapter," 1 Corinthians 13, the lecture has since become a classic.

Drummond studied for the ministry at the University of Edinburgh but graduated to become professor of natural science at the Free Church College in Glasgow. His book *Natural Law in the Spiritual World* attained greater popularity than many novels of the period. He traveled in England, America and Australia on both scientific and evangelistic missions.

The selections included in this volume from "The Greatest Thing in the World" and Drummond's other lectures illustrate the spiritual timelessness of the message of love.

Designed by Carole Muller.

Set in Baskerville, the fine transitional face named for the 18th century English printer John Baskerville of Birmingham.

Printed on Hallmark Eggshell Book paper.